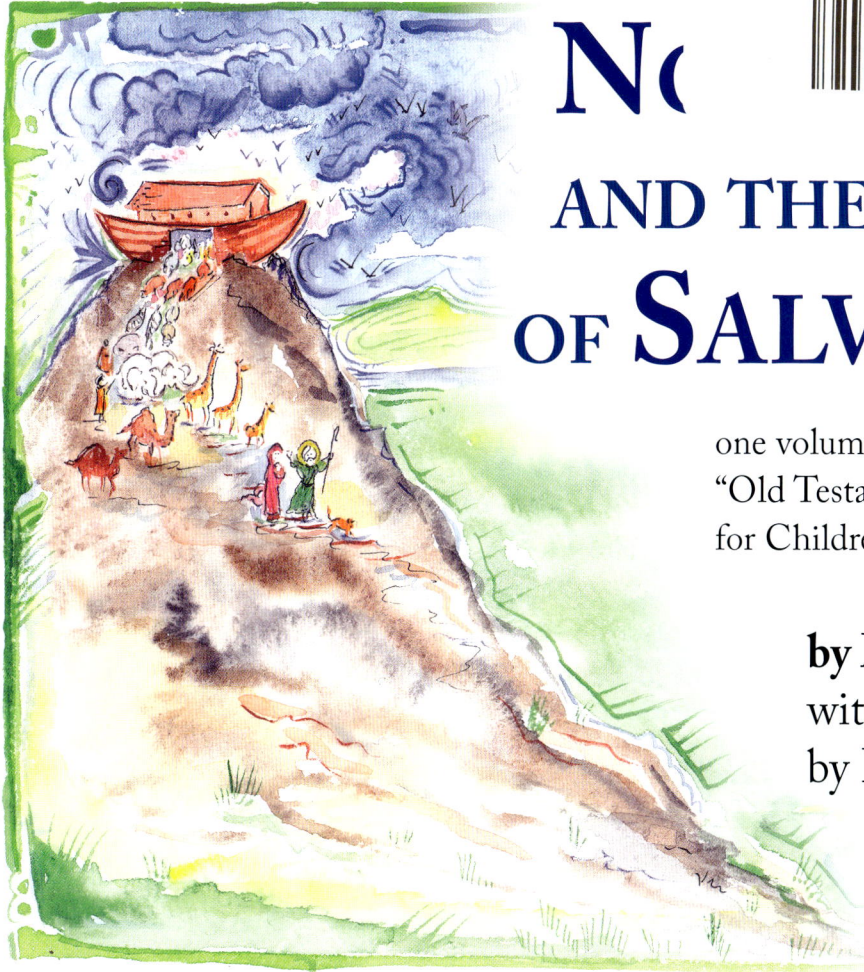

NOAH
AND THE ARK
OF SALVATION

one volume in the
"Old Testament Stories
for Children" series

by Mother Melania
with illustrations
by Bonnie Gillis

CONCILIAR PRESS
MINISTRIES, INC.
Ben Lomond, California

Noah and the Ark of Salvation
from the **Old Testament Stories for Children** series

Text © copyright 2009 by Mother Melania
Illustrations © copyright 2009 by Bonnie Gillis

Published by   Conciliar Press Ministries, Inc.
                 P.O. Box 76
                 Ben Lomond, California 95005

Printed in China

ISBN 10: 0-9822770-2-4
ISBN 13: 978-0-9822770-2-7

ABOUT THE "OLD TESTAMENT STORIES FOR CHILDREN" SERIES

Everywhere in the Old Testament, the Fathers of the Church see Christ, the Theotokos, and the Church revealed. The Fathers always understood the Old Testament in light of the New. Moses in the basket is a "type" of baptism. Jacob crossed his hands to bless Joseph's younger son (Ephraim) over his older son (Manasseh)—a prefiguring both of the Cross and of the surpassing of the Old Covenant by the New.

Using simple verse and colorful, semi-iconographic illustrations that are both sweet and reverent, the series aims to introduce children and their parents to the profound truths revealed in the pages of the Old Testament. Our hope is that the readers will develop a thirst to meet Christ in the Scriptures that so richly reveal Him.

ABOUT THE STORY OF NOAH

The Fathers tell us that Noah is a type as well as an ancestor of Christ. His name means "to give rest," and our ultimate rest is in Christ. Like Christ, Noah preached righteousness, was persecuted by those who would not repent, and saved those with him. The ark in which Noah, his family, and the animals were preserved from the water of the Flood typifies the Church, in which we are saved through baptism in water. The appearance of the dove is a foreshadowing of the coming of the Holy Spirit, who appeared in the form of a dove at Christ's Baptism and is received by each of the faithful in their own baptism. Noah's faith saved not just his family, but the animals. Likewise, through the children of God, the rest of creation—animals, plants, and inanimate things—will also be saved. The Flood also foreshadows the Last Judgment, when once again the wicked will perish and the righteous will be saved, this time for eternity.

You can find the full story of Noah and the Ark in the Book of Genesis, chapters 6 through 9.

Long ago in days of old,
When men in wickedness grew bold,
The Lord looked down and saw that they
Thought only evil—night and day.

Then God, on seeing how they'd strayed,
Said, "I am grieved that I have made
These men. Now, I'll blot out their race."
-—But Noah in God's sight found grace.

The Lord told Noah that He'd bring
A flood on earth, and everything
That breathed would die—but God would save
All those with Noah from the grave.

So God told Noah, "You shall make
An ark, and in it, you shall take
A pair of ev'ry beast and bird."
And he obeyed God's Holy Word.

He built the ark while other men
Continued doing evil. Then
The Lord told Noah, "I shall pour
A flood on earth in one week more."

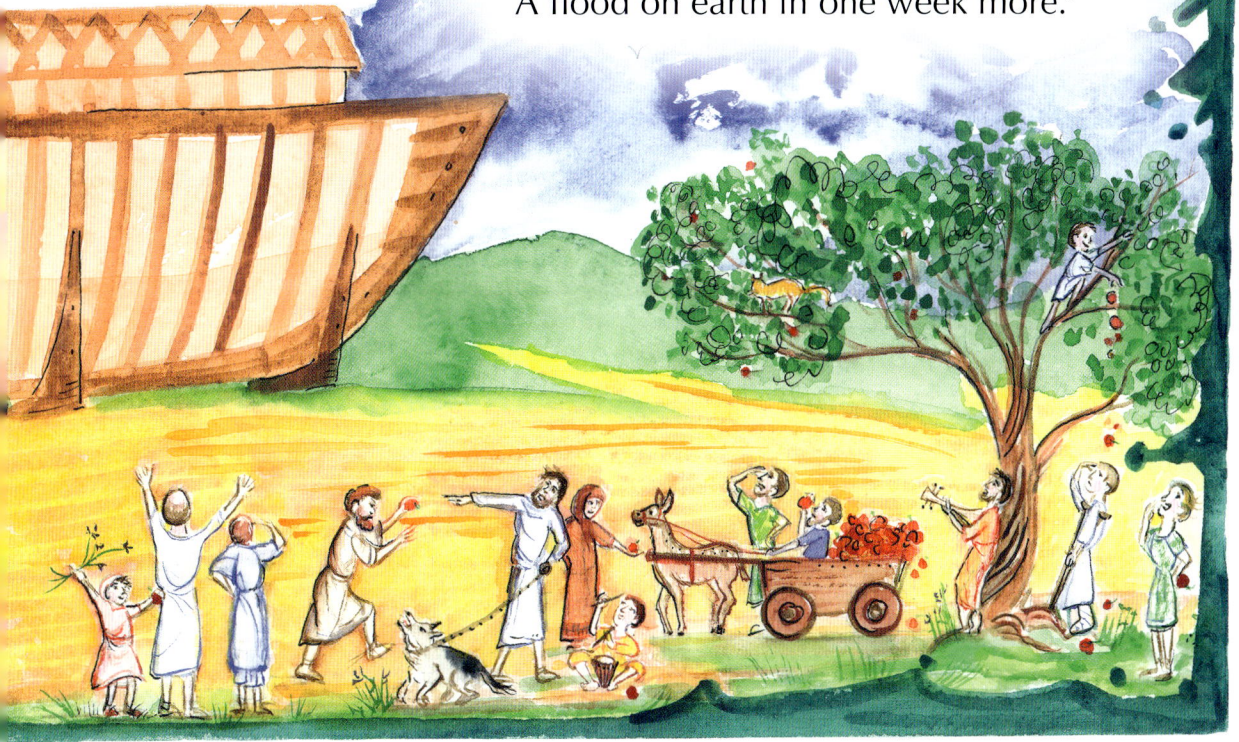

When Noah and his family, and
The birds and beasts,
   at God's command,

Into the saving ark all came,
God closed the door
and sent the rain.

It rained for forty days and nights.
The waters rose until no sight

Of land was left, and all outside
The ark were swept away and died.

The days went past.
     The months went by,
And still the waters
     rose up high,

But God remembered Noah, and
On Ararat the ark found land.

More time went by. Then Noah sent
A raven from the ark. It went
Up, up and flew around the sky
Until the face of earth was dry.

Then Noah sent a dove, but she
Could find no perch on land or tree.
So, as the day was growing dim,
The dove returned again to him.

Now Noah waited one week more
And sent the dove again. She bore
An olive twig to him—a sign
Of mercy and of peace divine.

He sent the dove again, but she
Did not return this time. So he
And ev'ry person, bird, and beast
Came out—from biggest to the least.

An altar Noah built, and when
He sacrificed upon it, then
The Lord said, "Never more will I
Cause ev'ry living thing to die."

"I place My bow up in the sky,
And this will be a sign that I
Will never flood the earth again,"
Said God, who loves both beasts and men.

By Noah's ark, Lord, Thou didst save
His fam'ly from a wat'ry grave.
And, baptized in Thy Church, are we
All saved from death to live in Thee.

Oh, Lord, may I like Noah heed
Thy Word and show my faith in deeds,
And when the floods of life are past,
May I find rest in Thee at last.

ABOUT THE AUTHOR AND ILLUSTRATOR

Mother Melania is a member of the community of St. Barbara Orthodox Monastery in Santa Paula, California.

An earlier series of her poems, *The Twelve Great Feasts for Children*, was published under the name of Sister Elayne, her name before she was professed as a stavrophor nun. She also has published a series of three books about Holy Friday, Holy Saturday, and Pascha, under the series title, *The Three-Day Pascha*.

Bonnie Gillis is an iconographer and illustrator who lives in Langley, British Columbia (Canada), where her husband, Father Michael, is pastor of Holy Nativity Orthodox Mission.

Bonnie was also the illustrator for both *The Twelve Great Feasts for Children* and *The Three-Day Pascha* series of books.